Dear Over-Stimulated Parent

10 small ways to save your sanity

Thank you Josh, Mom, and Dad - the best 3 parents I know.

Table of Contents

From Despair to Hope

I had just gotten my daughter strawberry-flavored frozen yogurt. Raleigh was 2, and though precocious, she was still an opinionated and stubborn toddler. We were late for an appointment. My body was tired from carrying my child, wrestling her in and out of her car seat, changing her diapers, and chasing after her all day. My head was spinning from the constant conversation with this little human I had created. She talked and questioned all day long - which I loved, but which also zapped my energy.

On this particular evening, Raleigh was refusing to get into her car seat. When she starting crying and fighting me, I snapped. It was the first time I remember raising my voice at my child. I shouted, “get in your seat!” And I’ll never forget the wide-eyed look she gave me. It was filled with concern and wisdom. She had never seen her mother like that, and she knew it wasn’t right. Instead of crying, she softly asked, “Mommy havin’ a hard time?” My eyes filled with tears because I couldn’t believe my 2-year-old had the emotional intelligence and compassion to ask me how I was doing. I apologized and swore to myself I would never raise my voice at my children again.

I’m sure you can guess how well I have kept that vow. (Not well). High-stress situations, a main ingredient of parenting, bring out the worst in us. Learning how to parent calmly and from a place of strength and compassion has been an uphill battle for me.

Raising children is a challenge for anyone, but when you add any extra ingredient–mental health issues, death, relationship troubles, a pandemic, loss of a job, special needs, trauma, sickness–raising well-adjusted children while remaining sane can seem impossible.

I became a mom at age 27. Before kids, I would have described myself as organized, responsible, social, and successful. But having children revealed needs I never knew I had. I realized that I required significant alone time to be a functioning member of society. Being the primary caregiver for small children also taught me that I could only handle so much touch, smell, and sound in a day before being sent into a panic attack. And I realized that it wasn't that I had always been such a great time-manager, I had just always had plenty of time to manage.

Taking stock of my strengths, weaknesses, and needs through the years has led me to create a toolbox of strategies for surviving parenthood and coming out on the other side with loved, healthy children AND my mental health intact. The ideas in this book are not meant as dogma, but rather as gentle suggestions. Take what you need, leave what you don't. These are the things that have helped me feel sane and fulfilled in an otherwise bleak and overstimulating time. I hope they do the same for you.

As you read these 10 strategies, I urge you to remember that a powerful tool we all possess is our perspective. As simple and uninspired as it may seem, reframing our circumstances can actually transform our lived experience. A shift in perspective can cause us to go from feeling defeated, hopeless, and unfulfilled, to feeling strong, content, and joyful. I don't say this to minimize the very real obstacles of mental health, finances, difficult relationships, or any other human trial that stands in the way of our peace. I believe that toxic positivity is a very real scourge in American pop psychology, and I never want to contribute to that. Physical and mental health should always be addressed first, by a doctor or therapist and medication, if needed. My whole reason for putting together this book is to assemble actual practical tools for tackling some of the physical hardships that plague parents. Just remember this...after you've done all you can to adjust your physical circumstances, a shift in personal perspective (if we can muster it) could be just enough to push you from despair to hope.

What Kind of Day?

How adjusting your expectations can transform your day from failure to success

You know the kind of morning. You intended to wake up early so you could make coffee, put on real clothes, and have a moment of silence before your children rose like loud, destructive phoenixes from the ashes of their bedclothes… but you ignored your alarm. Now, here you are at the late hour of 6:45am with what seems to be a hangover (even though you didn't drink last night) as multiple humans climb on top of you making alarmingly detailed breakfast orders at full volume.

Once you have stumbled out of bed and shaken the toddlers off your legs, you manage to put on a pair of pants and trip over toys into the kitchen. You make coffee first, in spite of the loud protests for breakfast, because you know that this routine will be even harder without it.

This, my friend, calls for a game-time decision: it's officially a "survival day." Early on in my parenting journey, I realized that not every day would be a golden twelve hour window of learning, cheer, productivity, bonding, and perfection. I mean, I thought I knew that before I had kids, but somehow I was still surprised when I found out that wasn't the case.

Somewhere along the way, I realized that my expectations about the day could greatly influence my actual experience of the day. In the beginning, if I had a day that wasn't "productive" and full of great learning opportunities for my kids, I would go to bed feeling defeated, bummed, and guilty. But as I gained a greater understanding about the responsibilities of a parent, I learned that there is absolutely no shame in a day spent keeping your kids fed, healthy, and loved. That's enough. So here's my solution for that gross guilt feeling: adjust your expectations.

When my first two children were 3 and 1, I remember a day when everything "went wrong." I was still a relatively new mom, and I hadn't learned how to adjust my expectations based on daily circumstances. That day, I woke up with the best of intentions. I planned to do a holiday craft with my kids, but the trip to Michael's was an absolute bust because we were all tired and cranky and the kids asked for everything in the store. Instead of making a nutritious lunch at home as I had planned, I pulled through the Chick-fil-a drive-thru. I spent nap time resting, but the rest was very unsatisfactory because I felt guilty the entire time for lying down instead of cleaning my disaster zone of a house. I ended that day feeling like a failure.

In hindsight, I understand that I would have felt completely differently about the day if I had only adjusted my expectations. If I had taken stock of how my family was feeling, I would have been less ambitious. Then, the failed Michael's trip, the Chick-fil-a run, and the chore-less nap time would have not seemed like failures at all. When I think back on my "worst" days as a parent, I realize that for many of them, adjusted expectations could have significantly altered my experience.

So here's how it looks to practice adjusting your expectations. When you wake up, evaluate how you're feeling. Are you depressed? Did you sleep well? Are you feeling healthy and motivated? Depending on how you're doing, decide if you're going to have a "survival day" or a "productive day." A productive day might look something like I had originally pictured. A day when you wake up early, do lots of housework, put kids in matching outfits, etc. You can be proud of your accomplishments at the end of a day like that! A survival day, on the other hand, is all about making it to bedtime in one piece. And you can be proud of a day like that too!

To understand what I mean, here are some sample schedules:

<u>Survival Day:</u>
Wake up when kids wake up
Cereal/something easy for breakfast

TV time for all
Take a walk (or not)
Change some diapers
Feed some babies
NAPTIME (even for big kids and the parent)
Kids play, parent supervises
Frozen pizza for dinner
BEDTIME

Productive Day:
Wake up early
Make coffee/eggs
Do some laundry
Take kids to the park
Run some errands
Change some diapers
Feed some babies
NAPTIME
Make some phone calls, answer emails
Make dinner (frozen pizza is still fine!)
BEDTIME

One of these days isn't better or worse than the other. "Surviving" is not a failure - it's a resounding success! And keep in mind that these are just examples. Maybe on your "productive day" you don't want to wake up early. That's fine! This exercise is all about setting an expectation for yourself. You get to decide what kind of day you're going to have - not me, not Dr. Oz, not anyone else.

This strategy is a case study for how reframing your expectations can drastically influence your "success" rate. Anecdotally, I have personally become a less stressed, more content individual than I was five years ago, even though my daily circumstances have changed very little. Setting a realistic goal for my lifestyle and productivity has trickled down into my mood, my relationships, and the atmosphere of my home.

Just remember: as long as you and your kids are happy and healthy, everything else is flexible. Intentionally setting expectations each morning can serve to dissolve the guilt that so often plagues parents. Knowing that you have accomplished all you set out to accomplish - even if that's just making it to bedtime in one piece - brings contentment and fulfillment.

Practical Application

Write your own sample schedules below

Survival Day	Productive Day
Morning Routine	Morning Routine
Afternoon Routine	Afternoon Routine
Evening Routine	Evening Routine

Learning Your Signals

Using messages from our bodies to minimize meltdowns

Our bodies are smart. They know that we are stressed before we do. Taking the cues that our bodies are sending us can help minimize the number of times we "lose it" with our kids. But as with all new information, there's a learning curve. It takes time and attention to understand how our bodies are communicating with us.

I could manage stress reasonably well before I had children. The regular demands of work, housekeeping, and relationships rarely sent me over the edge. This was because my physical needs were met. I was eating at normal times, resting when I needed to, and taking plenty of alone time. It was a shock to my system when I had children, became a stay-at-home mom, and was thrust into a reality where I had no alone time unless I painstakingly planned for it. So, just like many other parents, I started to feel burned out. I was often over-touched, over-stimulated, sleep-deprived, and falling apart.

Before I came to understand my body's signals, I would find myself in a pile on the floor after the constant demand of caring for small children had pushed me to the absolute limit. One morning, when I was very pregnant with my third child and had an even shorter fuse than usual, I was rushing around trying to get my two other kids ready for a preschool. I was trying to make lunches, get backpacks ready, and assemble everything for the day. My body was giving me all kinds of flashing red warning lights that I needed to take a moment of rest, but I didn't listen. And so, my body forced the issue. I ended up passed out on the couch for a half hour. Thankfully, the actual blackout was brief, so for most of that time I could hear and supervise my older two kids, but I was utterly unable to stand or carry on with the morning as planned.

When I wasn't listening to my body, my body would force me to take time to rest because I wasn't taking it for myself. This burnout didn't just hurt me, it also hurt my kids. The moments when I became overwhelmed were either times that I would crash from exhaustion, or the times that I would yell, lose my temper, and throw an adult tantrum. And then I would feel incredibly sad, because I knew how damaging that was for my children to witness. It was a terrible example of how an adult should manage their emotions.

Over time, I learned that my nervous system was sending me clear messages that could help prevent burnout from happening. Understand that they are different for everyone, but for me, I realized that when I was nearing my limit I would feel light-headed, irritable, and confused. I'm still not sure why my body responds this way to stress, but now I know that when I begin to feel that way, I need to take a personal timeout in order to prevent an explosive moment.

Timeouts are rarely convenient or ideal. In a perfect world, we could go into a sound-proof room for an hour to light some candles and meditate. Since that is unlikely to happen, we must make do with a compromise. Here are time out instructions:

1 - Make sure kids are safe. Older kids in front of a screen or playing in their rooms, baby in a crib or securely in a bouncer or other device

2 - Go into the quietest space in your house. For me, that's often the bathroom.

3 - If possible, put in headphones.

4 - Do whatever you want. Scroll social media, listen to a song, do a 5 minute guided meditation. Whatever will bring you back to a place of stability.

A frequent argument I hear when I suggest this strategy goes something like this: "but I can't relax when my kid is crying! It just makes me more stressed." And I understand and agree with that. BUT. Remember that the goal here isn't "relaxation" - the goal is calm. In order to achieve calm, we have to remove ourselves from the stressful situation, even if just for a moment. If you can hear children screaming, as long as you know they are safe, please don't be afraid to put in headphones and turn up some white noise, even for 60 seconds just so your blood pressure can creep back down. Will you become perfectly zen, and return to your children as a benevolent Mary Poppins? Certainly not. Will you return as a less yell-y, more rational version of yourself? Yes. And that is good enough.

Practical Application

Write your own timeout strategy below

When I'm feeling stressed, my body sends me these signals:
The next time I start to see these signals, I will make sure my kids are safe and go:
When I'm there, I will:

Daily Quiet Times

Using the routine of quiet time to establish order and reset emotions

Football players get half-time. Actors get intermission. School children get recess. And parents get nap time. Everyone knows that babies take naps, but a common misconception is that the respite of daily nap times has to disappear as kids get older.

I distinctly remember when my first child was a baby. I relied heavily on her daily nap times. When she was around 3 years old, she started showing signs that she was ready to drop her afternoon nap. That thought filled me with dread. Her nap time was the only quiet time I had to myself - time that I used to read, catch up on TV, be creative, or sleep - and the realization that that was all going to change made me anxious.

It was around that time that an older, wiser mother gave me some life-changing wisdom. She told me that, in her house, they still did daily nap times, even though her kids were much older than mine. She said, "It's good for them to have an hour or two of quiet. They're allowed to read or color, and I have some alone time."

From then on, I decided that quiet times would replace naps once my kids outgrew their need for an afternoon sleep.

Now, every day at 1pm, all three of my children go to their rooms. My 6 and 3- year-olds either rest, color, or play with a tablet, my 1-year-old naps, and I either rest, watch tv, or do something else that makes me feel refreshed. I'm not suggesting that this exact schedule should be adopted by every family, but I am suggesting that every home needs an established rhythm that includes rest.

It is a well-researched fact that humans require rest, and becoming a parent does not release you from that need. Whether you schedule a daily afternoon nap time in your home, a morning siesta, or even an early evening quiet time for everyone, I'm a firm believer that each family should build resting into their schedule.

A crucial part of getting this schedule to work for me personally is honoring the "rest" principle for myself. It can be tempting to use that quiet hour to catch up on laundry or dishes or organizing - and I have been known to cheat and be productive from time to time - but in general, I only use daily quiet times to rest. It's that important.

Practical Application

Write your own daily quiet time strategy below

What time of day can you set aside as a daily "quiet time:"
How will your children safely and solitarily spend this time (be creative if you have to):
How will you spend this time:

Tantrum Tricks

Practical ways to diffuse outbursts in the moment

It was a hot July afternoon, and I was holding my toddler's hand in Ikea. My parents, brother, sister-in-law, and sister were all with us. It was supposed to be a fun family outing for everyone, but it rapidly devolved into a parenting nightmare. I had promised my daughter that she could get one of the tiny $2 stuffed tigers from the kids' department, but for reasons unknown to me, she became unsatisfied with that arrangement. Once she started throwing a fit, I told her, "Ok, you're not getting anything then."

I took her hand and started to lead her away, and all hell broke loose. She was on the floor, screaming, sobbing, and hyperventilating...all in front of my entire family. I was mortified and filled with self-doubt. Was I doing the right thing? Was my family horrified at my awful parenting? All I could do was carry her, potato sack style, out of Ikea and straight to her carseat.

This is not necessarily a "parenting" book - but it is a book meant as a life preserver for overstimulated parents. And what is the most overstimulating experience for a parent? Almost certainly it is a tantrum. The paralyzing hopelessness of a parent during a public tantrum is unique and terrible. The shame, the stress, the judgment, the overstimulation - it can be one of the most overwhelming experiences for a mom or dad. And if you live with any personal issues like ADHD, introversion, or high-sensitivity, a tantrum can be an even more heightened stressor.

There are countless learned professionals who can help all of us understand the chemistry, psychology, and nuance of a child's emotions and behaviors, but I'm not here to do that. I'm here to help other overwhelmed parents survive the explosive and exhausting moments of little people, with both their children and dignity intact. Here are the four strategies I personally use to neutralize tantrums.

1 - Distraction

This sounds like a no-brainer, but bear with me. Kids are interested in the things that you're interested in. So if you pretend to be absolutely captivated by something, even in the midst of a tantrum, your child is likely to be intrigued and, at least momentarily, forget about the source of their distress (be it an uncomfortable shoe, a stick they can't part with, or a wet spot on their pants). This tactic requires some pretty convincing acting, so I will admit that my theater degree gives me an advantage here. (And is possibly its only practical use.) This strategy is the best one for tantrums that are thrown in public and when you're in a hurry or trying to get your kids in and out of the car. Again - really throw yourself into the bit, otherwise it won't work. (As we all know, kids are onto us.) The very tone of your voice should change - make it sound like you're not even talking to your kids anymore because you're so enthralled in what you're seeing. It should be as though you can't even see your kids now because you're so fixated on the spiderweb, or unusual truck, or rock that you think might be actual gold. It will definitely feel silly as you're doing it (and probably as if you deserve an Oscar), but for me, it works like a charm 9 times out of 10.

2 - Choices

A classic tool for deescalating tantrums is the presentation of choices. Maybe the child isn't allowed to have the object of their desire - another piece of cake, to avoid a nap, etc. - and often the opportunity to choose something on their own can feel empowering and will at least somewhat dissolve their frustration. An example of some choices you might offer your child:

- a snack or a story time before nap
- to go on a walk or play hide and seek in the backyard instead of wrestling the dog (that's a common one in my house)
- to choose what fruit to buy at the grocery store instead of the cheap toy they want

3 - Sensory Stabilization

When my son is “in his feelings,” sometimes the best thing I can do is sit with him and help bring him back to reality. This is a tool I learned from my therapist for helping me to stop disassociating in my own life. For a child, it can look like this: “What colors do you see? Do you see anything yellow? Can you touch this blanket? Does it feel soft to you? How does it feel on your cheek?” Grounding your child back into their 5 senses can help to restore order to the chaos of their big emotions.

4 - Change of Environment

Mothers and fathers have been using this tool for hundreds of years. I’ve heard it said this way: “put your child outside or in water to solve any of their problems.” That might be an overstatement, but there is some truth there. Sometimes, the most effective way to diffuse a tantrum is a change of scenery. Taking a walk, running a lap, or, my personal favorite, taking a “fancy bath” are all excellent ways to calm your child’s senses. In our house, the “fancy bath” is a sacred and cherished ritual. When a child has had a hard day or can’t seem to shake the blues, I will offer a bath full of bubbles with a special drink (usually it’s just juice with ice in it), some music, and candlelight. Every. Single. Time. My child emerges rosy cheeked and smiling. The “fancy bath” has been a godsend in our home. (Side note: the “fancy bath” also works wonders on adults. Just add wine.)

Practical Application

Write your own tantrum management strategies below

When do you experience tantrums the most with your child/children?
How can you plan ahead for these tantrums?
What strategy do you feel will be most frequently helpful for you?

Reset

Creative ways to give everyone a break when things become too overwhelming

During the coronavirus pandemic, stay-at-home life with small children became even more demanding and relentless. In years prior, I would schedule outings throughout the week to break up the days at home. Those outings offered structure, variety, and enrichment to our days. But during the pandemic our options became severely limited. In fact, they were pretty much zero. We could walk around our neighborhood or go to the grocery store.

On one of those endless days I remember sitting hopelessly on my couch while all three of my children screamed for various reasons, realizing that it was only 9am and we somehow all had to make it to bedtime. To an outsider that situation might sound mundane and easily endured, but for a tired, over-stimulated mom, it felt truly desperate. How was I going to keep all these humans alive and in decent spirits for another TEN HOURS?

I could only think of one thing to do. There was just one place where all my children were safely and ethically restrained while I was "free" - the car. I piled the kids into their carseats, closed the van doors, and leaned against the car. I breathed a heavy sigh of relief. Even thirty seconds standing outside my car felt like a moment of crystal clarity and hope. Armed with my thermos of coffee and my AirPods, I made an hour long loop around the city while listening to *Folklore*. Mercifully, my van has a DVD player, but this strategy would work with tablets, or coloring books and crayons.

The idea here is to occupy the children safely so that the parent can let their brain wander for a few minutes. So it isn't really necessary to be in a car. This principle could work on a long walk while kids ride their bikes, in a stroller, or in a wagon. It could even work while kids play on a playground. Basically, be creative and find a way to employ your children so that you can allow your adult brain a moment of rest.

Another way to achieve a this outcome is via playdates. In a post-pandemic world, arranging playdates with one or two other families in similar situations provides an ideal opportunity for parents to socialize and have adult time. The novelty of being with other children or in a different space occupies their attention long enough to provide a respite to their parents. If you can find someone in your area, trading babysitting is also an excellent way to accomplish the goal of a "reset." Once a week or every other week, adults can alternate keeping all the kids so that the other stay-at-home parent can have a morning off. My mother-in-law employed this system for years when her children were young and often reminisces about how rejuvenating and meaningful those mornings alone were for her.

These types of outings serve as a reset button for the overwhelmed parent. It is impossible to parent our children well when we are depleted, frazzled, and over-stimulated. And while it isn't always an option to take a spa day or a vacation, we can find workarounds that allow our souls to breathe. It is, I believe, critical that we do this. If we don't, we are offering leftovers to our family, not to mention doing a disservice to our mental health. Stress and exhaustion turn us into shells of who we used to be, instead of the vibrant, interesting people we actually are. Our children, partners, and indeed, ourselves, deserve the best version of us.

Practical Application

Write your own reset strategy below

What are some activities that safely restrain your kids and relieve your brain?
How can you implement these activities as pressure-relief valves for high pressure days?

Don't Do Housework, Make Your House Work

Freeing yourself from the tyranny of your living space

If I were to ask you what is one of the biggest contributing factors to your feelings of overstimulation, you might answer "mess." Parents deal with vastly more mess than the average person. It's because not only are you responsible for your own chaos, you are also responsible for the astounding chaos of small creatures who, arguably, are more wolf-like than human when it comes to cleanliness and hygiene. I don't need to tell you how exhausting and maddening it is to walk into a recently cleaned bedroom to find piles of toys, broken crayons, and spilled water. It's almost as if our kids know what will cause our senses to short-circuit, and then do those exact things.

In addition to the excess disaster created by children, society has imposed some truly impractical housekeeping expectations on parents. If I did every chore that society has taught me will make my home functional and aesthetically pleasing, I would get up at 6am and work nonstop until dinnertime every single day. And, call me crazy, but that's not my idea of a fun or fulfilling life. I only get a few brief years on this planet, and I refuse to spend the bulk of them tidying my living space.

While I am committed to not being a slave to my house, I do recognize that as a stay at home mom of 3, the majority of household tasks fall to me. If I don't wash clothes for my kids, they won't have anything clean to wear. If I don't occasionally load the dishwasher, we won't have any clean plates. In addition to those daily needs, I have a certain amount of vestigial personality programming that has been derived from an upbringing full of leftover notions about a "woman's role" and how a house is "supposed" to look.

All of these factors make it difficult for me to practically live out my resolution to avoid bondage to housework every moment of the day. Even when I intentionally choose to sit down and rest, the undone cleaning taunts me and gives me a great deal of stress. How can I relax if I'm sitting in crumbs, or can't find a clean glass with which to have a drink of water?

So how do we live in a home that is safe, functional, and yet also not our cruel task-master? The lesson that I have been trying to internalize is this: my house should work for ME, and not vice versa.

This book does not set out to arm you with a new cleaning regimen that will revolutionize your life. I'm not going to teach you a magical method for folding clothes or scrubbing your sink. (There is a list of resources at the end of the book if you need some cleaning guidance.)

Instead, I seek to help you shift your perspective. Our experience of our home is drastically influenced by our expectations about what our homes should be. If we believe that our houses should be bright, trendy, and squeaky clean, then a cluttered, un-sexy space will feel a lot like failure.

BUT. If we believe that our house should be a place of comfort, rest, and functionality, then a cluttered, un-sexy space can simply feel like home. With that perspective in mind, I decided to identify the areas of my house and routine which were causing me the most stress, trouble-shoot those areas, and go from there.

Example: every morning I have to take a few different medicines. It doesn't sound like a big deal, but when you have 3 kids who need to be fed, changed, and placated first thing in the morning, fishing pills from 5 different bottles can be incredibly frustrating. In order to eliminate this unnecessary stress in my morning routine, I got a 30-day pill dispenser. At the beginning of the month, I spend 10 minutes portioning out my meds for the month. Now, instead of 2 or 3 high-intensity minutes, this task takes about 15 seconds of my morning.

Another example involves my kids' outfits for the week. It was too stressful to search for 3 different outfits every morning, so I bought some cheap hanging closet shelves.

Now, at the beginning of each week, I take 5 outfits out of the laundry for each kid, put them on the appropriate shelves, and during the week the kids can get their own clothes out without any help.

These small changes had nothing to do with a chronic need for my house to look better or more appealing, but instead they were made with the express intent of easing some of my burden. When I began to look at housework in this way, my home didn't seem so overwhelming or impossible. I still have lots of unresolved stress spots in my housekeeping routine. My laundry remains a source of anxiety for me, but I know I just haven't found the right solution yet. However, I don't let it discourage me or define my worth as a wife and a mother.

Another tool I rely on (especially during the lockdowns of 2020), is cleaning days. Every couple of weeks or so, I will send my kids out with my husband. They will go to the beach or the park, and I will have about 3 hours of uninterrupted cleaning time. I don't know about you, but I can clean pretty much anything in 3 hours. Having days like this on the schedule are a great source of comfort for me as I know that, even if the state of my house is becoming overwhelming, I'll get a chance to start all over by doing a deep clean on a designated day,

Practical Application

Brainstorm your own home stress relieving strategies below

What are 3 "problem areas" for you? (chores that cause unnecessary stress on a regular basis)
Write out a simple strategy for how you might tackle these areas. Are their organization tools that might help? A change of routine?
What are some household chores that society has made you believe you have to do, but that you could safely live without? In other words, what corners can you cut to minimize your housework stress?

Making Deposits When You Can

How to ensure emotional connection with your kids even you struggle with overstimulation

My three-year-old loves to cuddle. At least 10 times a day I will hear his little voice saying, "I want MO-mmy time. I want MO-mmy time." (That means he wants to wallow on my lap and watch Paw Patrol). And even though I prayed for children who were cuddle bugs, I find myself stressed by these requests at times. Overstimulation in the form of noise, mess, breastfeeding, hunger, etc., can leave cuddling (and other forms of physical contact :D) pretty low on my list of priorities.

But I have learned from older moms to know that one day I will DEFINITELY miss my snuggle times with him. How do I mitigate my son's need for cuddles with my need for less stimuli? Here's the answer: *I initiate cuddles* when I have enough gas in the tank.

I have learned to take note when I am rested, fed, and relatively low stress. In moments when I realize that cuddling actually sounds great to me, I will seek out my son and ask *him* to cuddle with *me*. (He never says no, God love him). This way, I am making those crucial deposits of physical touch, but at a time when doing so won't cause my blood pressure to spike.

I apply this same principle with my 6-year-old. She prefers quality time to cuddles - she wants to chat, read books, and do crafts - all of which can be draining. I have learned to initiate those activities with her myself when I am feeling up to it. I've also learned that she feels special just when she gets to run an errand alone with me, so as often as possible I will go on a solo run with her to the grocery store.

I call this "making deposits." Just as we can't make a deposit into our bank account if we don't have any money, we can't make relational deposits into our children when we are in an emotional or physical deficit. The discipline here is being self-aware enough to understand your own needs and moods. It takes some practice. Ultimately, giving to our children when we aren't depleted means that we we can give them intentional, meaningful attention, instead of reluctant, distracted attention.

There are undoubtedly going to be times when I will have to make emotional "withdrawals" on my relationship with my children. Discipline, consequences, and declining their requests all feel like withdrawals to them. That's why having a pre-paid account of deposits built into my relationship with them is crucial. It helps to balance out the less affectionate duties of parenthood so that my children never doubt their emotional connectedness with me.

There are definitely still times when I find myself stressed out by my son's cuddles or my daughter's questions. But being the one to initiate connective moments with them has helped me to ensure that I am building a foundation of positive moments with my kids that are meaningful not just for them, but for me too.

Practical Application

Write your own strategy for making deposits below

What makes your child/children feel loved?
When do you feel most energized and able to "make deposits" into your relationship with your child?
What is a creative way you can plan on making regular deposits into your relationship with your child?

Calm Corner

Building peace into your living space

Do you ever find yourself in a strange corner of your house, hiding from chaos? Maybe you lift your head out of your hands and realize that you're squatted down in the baby's nursery, or a closet, or maybe even outside. Have you ever wondered why you end up in those random places during moments of stress?

Over-stimulated people need dedicated physical space in which to decompress. Knowing this about yourself isn't being "extra" or "needy," it's being wise and strategic so that you remain sane for yourself and your family.

My theory is that over-stimulated parents seek out the part of their house that feels the calmest and most orderly. I remember locking myself in the playroom during lunchtime one day. Why? Because I had just cleaned it and the rest of the house was, as usual, trashed. I sat on a clean couch in a tidy, quiet room so I could collect my thoughts and clear my senses.

Once I understood this pattern in my behavior, I realized that I could help my future stressed self. I created an adult "calm corner" for myself. (I have a calm corner for my kids too.) I chose the most likely space - my bedroom - and made sure that, as often as possible, it was neat, peaceful, and available for me to come and decompress. I used blackout curtains - not because I think they're the most stylish, but because I needed less stimuli. There are plenty of pillows on the bed, a phone charger always plugged in beside the bed, my headphones charged and readily accessible, and my favorite painting hanging right beside my side of the bed.

Now, when I need a moment away from the sights, sounds, and smells of 3 children, I excuse myself to the oasis of my bedroom.

When I have suggested this strategy to people, I have often heard the argument "doesn't that make your kids feel abandoned or hurt their feelings?" I hear and understand the heart of that objection. Secure attachment is crucial to the healthy development of little people. That is why communication is critical. Children are always learning. They are training to be adults. And because of this, it does not serve them well to hide our needs from them. Masking our overstimulation not only causes speedy burnout for us as parents, it also teaches our children that having needs is not normal. They will grow up with an emotional blind spot - believing that well-adjusted adults shouldn't need breaks or alone time.

I am NOT saying that we should express frustration with our children or make our alone time about them. Causing them to believe that they are the source of our stress and discomfort is not helpful either. So here is an example of how to explain your needs to your child: "I am going to take some alone time. Sometimes, I need time by myself to make sure I'm a good mom. I'm setting a timer for 5 minutes, and I will turn a show on for you. You may not bother me unless it's an emergency until I come out in 5 minutes. I love you. I'll be right back."

This is not a perfect system and, as with anything else, it takes practice. Your children may have to experience this process several times before they fully understand and accept it. But at the end of the day, you are not only preserving your mental health, you are raising a well-adjusted human who understands the importance of taking care of themselves because they saw it modeled consistently by their caregiver.

Practical Application

Write your own strategy for creating a calm corner below

What space in your home can you dedicate as your calm corner?
What changes can you make to that space so that it is always peaceful and inviting for you?

Little Boundaries

Building a buffer between chaos and your mental health

I had just had my first baby. She was so lovely. So terrifyingly small and amazingly perfect. I was obsessed with her and I held her every second I could. So, as with many first time moms, my self-care suffered. Once my husband went back to work and I was alone with her during the day, my nails never got done, I rarely used the bathroom alone, and my true showers were few and far between. I remember gently placing my daughter in a Moses basket on the floor of my tiny bathroom so I could peek from behind the shower curtain to make sure she was ok while I rushed through washing and rinsing my hair. Many times she would cry during the entire shower, causing cortisol to pump through my veins and reinforcing the idea that I was being selfish in my self-care.

This lifestyle is sustainable for a little while. The parenting survival mode of having a newborn is both exhausting and exhilarating, but it can't last forever. When a baby is between 6 months and a year old, parents have to find some kind of "new normal" in order to remain happy and healthy. A mistake many new parents make (me included) is that they exist in some quasi-survival mode long after their baby is born. New moms and dads will often continue to de-prioritize their own basic needs, creating the perfect conditions for burnout.

As I have added children over the years, I have learned to look for places to build healthy boundaries with them. Again, this doesn't mean that I am abandoning our children, or communicating to them that their presence is a bother or an inconvenience. It simply means taking care of my own basic needs while also showing them what it looks like to build healthy habits and relationships.

My personal boundaries include pooping alone, showering alone, not getting up again from my meal once I have given everyone their food and drinks, and consistent bedtimes each night so my partner and I can have alone time. Here are some healthy ways to phrase these boundaries to kids:

- "I'm using the bathroom right now. We all need privacy in the bathroom. I will be out in a few minutes when I'm done."
- "I'm taking a shower right now. Please go play quietly for a few minutes and I will come read a book to you when I'm done with my shower."
- "I have already given you your food and drink. I will not be getting up to get Ranch dressing right now because mom needs to eat too. You may get it yourself if you would like."
- "We do bedtime just like this every night. You must stay in your bed and rest right now. It's important that your dad and I hang out after bedtime. I love you! Goodnight."

During the vast majority of the day, the kids know I am available to talk, get them snacks, take them on walks, read to them, and bathe them just to name a few. While stating these boundaries does require an adjustment for them, it does not deprive them of my time, attention, or care. When children are secure and loved, these types of boundaries will only reinforce the stability of their relationship with you, and instill in them important relationship skills.

Practical Application

Write your own strategy for establishing little boundaries below

List 3 boundaries you need to establish:
Write out some positive ways to phrase these boundaries that emphasize your own needs without placing a burden on your children:

Pick Your Things

Prioritizing for the life you want instead of the life society expects of you

You've probably seen that meme that says something like "How am I supposed to stay hydrated, go to work, eat 3 meals a day, pay my bills, exercise, mail Christmas cards, not do crack, keep up with my tv shows, get 8 hours of sleep, go on dates, and have a skincare routine?" I repost it every time I see it because it perfectly captures the ludicrous expectations of the so-called American Dream.

Every day I scroll through Instagram, and every day I un-follow a blonde lady with a blow-out, a plaid scarf, and a big over-decorated house. No shade to her - I'm sure she's lovely - but seeing her perfectly staged photos merely reinforces the litany of absurd "goals" I seem to be expected to have for my life.

There is nothing wrong with wanting your kitchen cabinets to be beautifully organized, with your cereal in clear acrylic containers and your spices in Joanna Gaines inspired canisters. If that makes you happy and you have the bandwidth to make that happen, then by all means, buy a label maker and go to town. BUT. Don't you dare feel guilty if your cabinets are crammed with cardboard, plastic, and ugly packaging because you don't have the time or energy to make it more aesthetically pleasing.

Something that has helped me to neutralize the guilt and self-doubt of just existing as an adult woman in America is to *pick my things.* This means that I took the time to intentionally decide what "things" I wanted to prioritize in my life. I knew I couldn't do it all, so what was *actually* important to me? What were the things that would make me happy, peaceful, and proud of myself?

What are "things" you might ask? For the purposes of this chapter I am working with the very technical and official definition of: "the values and activities on which I spend most of my time and energy." I made a list of the values and tasks that I saw as important for my lifestyle and parenting. For example, here are some of my lifestyle "things:"

- Creativity (writing, creating content, photography)
- Physical activity (yoga, cycling)
- Relationships (intentional time once or twice a month w my partner and/or close friends)
- Activism for racial and gender equality
- Learning (reading, listening to podcasts, researching)
- Mental health and spirituality (therapy, meditation, church, prayer, music)

These are the ideas and activities where you will find me spending most of my time. My Instagram posts, my Facebook conversations, and my free time all revolve around these items. This might not seem especially revelatory, so please notice the things that are NOT on this list:

- Home decorating
- Cooking
- Environmentalism
- Cleaning
- Fashion/shopping

This doesn't mean that I don't do or support those things, it just means that they aren't "my things." I still decorate my house when I feel up to it or if I get the urge, but I don't make it a priority or build it into my daily life. I recycle and practice sustainability when I can, but it is not a primary focus of my life at the moment. I like new clothes and looking fashionable, but those just aren't the most important things to me at this stage of my life.

Now, here are some of my parenting "things:"

- Emotional connection (ALWAYS priority 1)
- Identity and confidence building
- Self-worth and spirituality
- Race and gender equality

- Reading
- Creativity
- Nature

Here are some things that aren't on my personal parenting priority list:

- Closely-monitoring screen time
- Eating clean
- Cute, fashionable clothes
- Toys
- Extra curricular activities

None of the items in this second list are bad, in fact, they are all great things to focus on! But I know that I don't have room in my life to prioritize all the items in both lists. I just don't possess the mental, physical, or emotional capacity to micro-manage that many details. Of course I will occasionally tell my kids to turn off the screens, but because I prioritize nature, emotional connection, and reading, I'm not going to stress about the exact number of hours they spend in front of the TV. Of course I will make sure they eat vegetables and protein, but organic ingredients is not something I have the time or money to make a top priority.

Intentionally "picking your things" can give you a great deal of freedom. Releasing yourself from the guilt of accomplishing every single item on the long list of things social media and experts tell you to do frees you up to be passionate and present for the things you *actually* care about. Doing a few things well, whether it be in our lifestyle or in our parenting, is far preferable to doing everything crappily. Write that on my tombstone.

Practical Application

Brainstorm your own “things” below

Pick at least 5 lifestyle things:

Pick at least 5 parenting things:

My parenting philosophy could be summed up as: "cut yourself some slack." A lot of internet trolls like to shame parents like me for being lazy, or tell me that I'm putting my own needs ahead of my kids. And to them I say this: you obviously don't know me. Getting to a healthy place of self-care, boundaries, and intentionality has taken lots of years, therapy, and effort. This is because my default setting is to be the haggard martyr who never eats, never sleeps, never exercises, and never takes time for herself.

I finally realized that this regimen was not serving me or my children. It was, in fact, robbing them of what they really needed: a happy, self-actualized mom who could give them couch cuddles without cringing, laugh with them in the floor without worrying about how clean my kitchen counters were, and give my deepest love and affection to them from a place of authenticity and joy.

Most parents I know are conscientious and deeply concerned with the well-being of their children. (If you are not, then this book isn't for you). Learning and understanding your own needs is only going to make you a better parent. It isn't going to take you away from your children or turn you into a selfish Stepford wife (or husband or partner). Love yourself, love your kids, pick your things, and go be free.

Additional Resources

Parenting/discipline:

- The Whole Brain Child by Daniel Siegel
- Parenting with Love and Logic by Foster Cline and Jim Fay
- No Drama Discipline by Daniel Siegel and Tina Pay Bryson
- Cribsheet by Emily Oster
- Screamfree Parenting by Hal Runkel
- How to Stop Losing Your Sh*t with Your Kids by Karla Naumburg
- Boundaries with Kids by Henry Cloud and John Townsend
- The 5 Love Languages of Children by Gary Chapman
- Don't Mom Alone podcast
- FAM: For All Moms podcast

Cleaning/housekeeping:

- How to Keep House While Drowning by KC Davis
- The Life-Changing Magic of Tidying Up by Marie Kondo
- Cleaning Sucks by Rachel Hoffman
- A Slob Comes Clean podcast

About Bree

Bree Card is a skeptical, introverted, creative mom of three children, Raleigh (6), Boone (3), and Ezekiel (1). Bree's husband/high school sweetheart Josh is a medical device sales rep, and Bree made the move from career-woman to stay-at-home mom/photographer/writer when her second child was born. The jarring transition spurred a permanent therapy slot on Tuesdays, a marriage meltdown, and a crisis of faith. A few years in survival-mode served as an awakening. Now, Bree is passionate about bringing reason, science, and care for mental health to the world of parenting.

Between the grueling and beautiful hours spent caring for her children, Bree enjoys snuggling Sully (Newfoundland mix), drinking IPAs, reading classic literature, studying pop culture, and spending quality time with a select few.

Made in United States
North Haven, CT
02 February 2023